Screaming
Olives

Screaming
Olives

Farid Bitar

STACK
BOOKS

Smokestack Books
1 Lake Terrace, Grewelthorpe,
Ripon HG4 3BU
e-mail: info@smokestack-books.co.uk
www.smokestack-books.co.uk

ISBN 9781838198800

Smokestack Books
is represented by
Inpress Ltd

for Palestine
my lover

for Gladys Goris
my soul mate

to all the known
and unknown
killed by the wars
in Palestine

Contents

Introduction

This collection of poems is dedicated to the Palestinian resistance and resilience against the occupation. This occupier is relentless, set on destroying and erasing Palestinian existence from the land between the river and the sea.

I am a Jerusalemite born in 1961, when the Jordanians ruled the West Bank and Jerusalem. In 1967 I witnessed the war which came walking to my sleepy Jericho. King Hussein of Jordan ordered his troops to pull out and struck a deal behind the scenes with the Israelis, betraying Jamal Abdel Nasser, leader of the Arab world. We lived in Jericho – by the time my parents reached Jerusalem to see the rest of our family, 17 Napalm bombs had dropped on the Indian Hospice in the old city, which left three of my relatives dead and ten badly burned. That war scarred me for life.

I witnessed more wars after that. I survived the first Intifada in 1987 and moved to New York City, just to try to live a peaceful life. But that was a dream that would not let me be. The small-scale wars never stopped – three major invasions in Gaza, and so many other situations. The killing never stops. It haunts me at night, when I mostly write.

I refuse to be erased.

Farid Bitar
New York 2021

Foreword

Not simply a cry of anguish, though it is that too, *Screaming Olives* contains raw fruits of wisdom plucked from decades of a painful and violent history – the history of the state of Israel's attempted erasure of Palestine from the world map. This seemingly intractable geopolitical conflict dominates global headlines as an endless war – though the mainstream media generally neglect to mention that only one side has an army, not to mention nuclear weapons and the financial backing of a superpower, while the other endures impoverished lives under a settler-colonial apartheid regime. The catastrophe wrought by the creation of Israel is fundamentally though a human conflict, rooted on both sides in trauma: a collective trauma, transplanted from Europe into Palestine, that can only be healed by a just peace grounded in human rights. One of those rights is the right to speak one's truth. If the power of poetry stems from its ability to express the complexity of emotional truths, then in the stark absence of a political peace process, poetry's role is more important than ever: to share personal truths with friends, family and strangers – even 'the enemy' – and in so doing generate awareness, encourage empathy and help heal the individual writer and reader.

Although bristling with political detail, and urgently calling for change, *Screaming Olives* is not a manifesto, but a restless creative response to dislocation, dispossession and colossal injustice. A child victim of war, witness to carnage and forced into exile, Farid S Bitar has become a writer, painter, activist and a man of faith, his consciousness a palimpsest of cultures, languages and aesthetic vernaculars. His poems invoke the wounded child and the Sufi mystic, the American Beats, Cavafy and Anna Akhmatova, graffiti and hip hop artists, his Jewish 'cousins' and a Druze lover, Arab writers from al-Mutannabi to Dareen Tatour, bringing all these disparate perspectives to bear on the Palestinian experience of loss, brutality, and abandonment, the suffering of Gaza and the political prisoners; but also of survival, resistance and solidarity, the diasporic grassroots, the suburban commute, Black Lives Matter. There's a chaotic energy to Bitar's voice, charged as it is with anger and grief, yet his poems also turn on a sharpened dime, in the midst of their fury glinting with humour or spinning off into yearning reflection. Sincere and vulnerable to the core, Farid S. Bitar tells it as it is, bluntly sharing his pain, while also conjuring sensual images of the past: childhood memories which summon him like mirages, the Ithaka of his Jerusalem, a dream of justice that can never and will never die.

Naomi Foyle

Above the Clouds

How do I write a poem?
While I am above the clouds
How do I sing with a bird?
A sonata to my beloved
Or my lost land twirling in dust?
How do I touch a cloud?
From my plane window
50,000 feet above
Shapes estranged
Crystalized

Looking into a mirage
Remembering Andalusia
Remembering Alhambra
That was where I came from
I am still resilient
I scream in my mother's tongue

I raised my flag in front of
The Waldorf Astoria Hotel, NYC
Green, Black, White and Blood
Where Ashkenazi is dining
The mastermind of a Gaza massacre
A thousand dollars a plate
A thousand fools attending
To raise more money
To kill more Palestinians
Criminalized

I envy how clouds get along
Raining down on the misery of this mad world
I wish they drop acid rain on Zion
I think of the Umayyad dynasty
I think of Tareq Ibn Ziyad
I think of Palestine before Nakbah time
I wish those days come back
Harmonized

I woke up with my head twisted
Staring into the clouds outside
Wishing my plane would land
In my garden of Jerusalem
The one that got bombed an eternity ago
But that's another dream of mine.

Handalah

in memory of Naji al-Ali

A man approached
Intruding on my space
Out of the blue moon
Asking
Boy, where do you come from?
Oblivious to the beast
I exclaimed
Where do I know you from?
Persisting with the demand
I replied
From my mother's thing
His face frowned angrily
I corrected myself
God created me I think
Actually, I am from the land
Of milk and sunny
I am a sabrah-Handalah
The cactus with thorns
I am the other Semite though
The man perplexed
So you are not the chosen one
Yes I am
The indigenous one
Silence fell
He departed mumbling under his breath
What a crazy dude
I was ecstatic
I pondered
The last time we hosted a stranger
He took over the house.

Upstream

Rowing downstream
Being one with – water – hummingbirds
& the static of the human
At the river banks
HIGH-LOW

I spot huge fish at the bottom
I spot fish heading the wrong way
I spot hundreds of fish belly up
I need an oxygen tank to breath
From all the rotting stink

Feeling overwhelmed
I turn my kayak upstream
The current keeps taking me
Downstream
Passing migrants crossing
The Rio Grande
Heading North of the border
Away from Trump's wall
Shouting obscenities

I decide to disembark
Walk a mile
Reminiscing Selma & Martin.
Barefoot logging my kayak
On a very harsh bedrock
Bottom of my feet turn
Black & Blue
Low-Low

Determined to reach my destination
Upstream
Finally I lose my sense of direction
With all the salmon
Committing a mass exodus
Dying in a shallow bend of the river.
Just after laying their eggs.

Bedouin Beauty

Dark but not stirred
By my tears
The world is fluttering
Over the dead
I complain to you
I cry from my pain
I am stinking drunk
I am choking on my
Bloody tears
I bitch to myself
About the status of the Universe
But no one listens
Neither Netanyahu
Nor Mubarak
Nor Obama
But Osama
That's a different case.

O! Dark beauty of the desert
My eyelids are blinking
Twitching-fluttering
Over the dead in Gaza and beyond
Over the Iraqi civilians
They called them collateral damage
I hate that term
It's insulting to the human

I cry to you my dark beauty
You just keep staring at me
With your killer Bedouin black eyes
At least you listen.

Hicks Town

A man in transition
Choosing to be direct
About 'intensifications & ramifications'
While another twists & turns
Bashing a poor man's head
A nomad in disposition
Getting on board with the composition
'Yara, yara, yara.
Which one do you prefer???

I am an Anarchist
I belong to no one
Even the almighty complains
I am a nomad from Hicks Town
Seeking an Inquisition of a kind
About that 'Right of Return'
Who stays put & who goes out
I guess the Talmudic Judaism
Will have to decide
While Zion keeps gobbling my leftover land
While Zion keeps erasing my behind

I don't need permission
To dwell in my father's land
In Al-Qatamon – West Jerusalem that is
Because I know it's going to be
My final resting space
If not, Jericho will suffice for now
In my peripheral I observe
The Anglo Saxon
The frowning with a twist of lime
When my name comes upside down
O! Mohammad where art thou
Home grown bombs on the rise
Tired of this Hicksville town
Need to ditch me this Amreeka
And fly away to another Shika Beeka.

Red Red-Green Green

broken down hearts
broken down dreams
broken down hopes
no one will ever break my will
Roaming streets of rubble
diving into tunnels of Rafah
chanting Green-Green
No, Red-Red
I am Black September
I am popular front
I am Habash
I am Ahmad Jibril
I am the Phoenix rising
I am fertile
Keep burning my babies
I am Green-Green
Raining down missiles
On Tel-Aviv with expensive condos
Soon on your Keenest in Jerusalem

Netanyahu, watch that hair weave
From taking off on a Ben-Gurion runway
Keep promising your chosen people
To make sure you get re-elected
keep committing crimes against humanity in Gaza
hope you enjoy your nightmares
looking at pictures of dead children.

Red Red
Green Green
Popular resistance
Palestine in between.

Vision of Hope

I am Black September
Born in the Jordanian camps of 1970
The camps will be reborn in
Haifa – Yaffa – Galil & Akka
Watch out for my venomous bite

I wear red on my chest
The blood of my fallen comrades
I see green fields of Jenin in the distance
Across from the Eretz fence of Gaza
Where the IDF soldiers are sniping

My fellow farmers harvesting their fields
I see white hope, I never will ever give up
I see my dream in Jerusalem materializing
I see the walls of the West Bank tumbling down

Where my fellow Palestinian brother and mother
Are praying at the Dome of the Rock peacefully
Where I can live in dignity in the Jewish Quarter
In my father's demolished house of '74

One day my soul will dwell eternally in Falasteen.

Charcoals

Crossing the mahsoom-cinder blocks
From Ramallah into Jerusalem
Soldiers boarded the bus
Screaming get off
Collect your belongings
A search ensued
A blonde soldier
No more than twenty
Screaming
'He has a set of knives'
Came out from her
Hell hole
Brandishing an M-16
Screaming again
Open your knapsack
And show us your knives

I panicked
My heart dropping
Below zero inferno
I said, 'It's only my set of charcoals
That I brought
To add some colour
To this war-ravaged town'

Soldier extremely disappointed
That I am not a mercenary killer
Still remembering the Yemini soldier
who came to my aid
laughing cynically at blondie

I was saved but only this time around.

Return

I will return one day
I will utter unbelievable words of joy
My father's key with me still
To his house an eternity ago
My family also with me
I will return – we will return
I will knock on the door
Mother still waiting there
I lost my father
Don't know where
I will ring the churches' bells
I will pray in the Dome of the Rock
Like I used to
Mother asked: where is your father?
She was yearning
She was pacing
I replied: I lost my father
She demanded that I look for him
I stated, don't worry he will return
I will pray on the wall
And tell Suhyoon to GO
I will bring down that ugly wall
When are you coming back?
I asked Jerusalem
When, when...
O! JERUSALEM

In My Sleep

My life passed me by
My destiny, my wisdom
My years are spent reaching out
My fate came visiting – in my sleep.
My love has evaporated into a velvet sky

A ghost dropped me a note of
Abstention and apprehension
A dear friend injured my inner soul

An enemy came by
I said to him with conviction
What do you seek from me!
And what are you doing in my dream?

In my broken ribs,
In my jurisdiction,
In my swollen veins,
    my face is buried in her breast

I am frozen in my time,
I am burning in my sleep,
I am petrified in my space,
I am running into destruction.

Charlie Hebdo

I am holy
I am Charlie
I am nameless
I am shameless – faceless
They will never break my pencil down
They will never break my voice out
Paris united
40 countries
14 heads of states
Je suis Charlie
Donne-moi ma liberté
I am not ISIS – never will be
I wonder what Netanyahu is doing here
Walking the line
Wish he learns
From this world unity
A million and more
Wish we all learn from the line.

Knocking

I am facing a door
In a velvet sky
Tormented – besieged
Hoping someone will let me in
Still knocking on Balfour's head
Not Clapton style
'Knocking on heaven's door'
But rather Roger Waters style
Also Muddy Waters style
200 years of slavery
In god bless America
Not really
Finally a European woman
Answered the door
She was shouting
'What do you want?
O! It's you again,
Didn't I tell you to get lost?
There's nothing left.'

I replied: 'Yes it's me again; I brought the rest of my family.'

I always come back
I mean we never left.

Who Am I?

Am I a Semite?
Or Anti-Semite?
How did it all start?
How did we get to this mess?
How did it all go so wrong?
What is wrong with this picture?

Give me a moment
While I adjust the outer limits
Into the twilight zone.
Let me take you back in time
To the land of Canaan,
The land of my fathers,
Abraham, Ishmael and Isaac,
The land of sacrifice, *Al-Tadd-hiyha*.
And who was sacrificed?
Who's wrong and who's right?
Whose Promised Land is it?

I know that I am a Semite Arab,
Descendent of Ishmael (Ishmael).
My cousin the Jew is a Semite too.
Descendent of Yitzhak (Isaac);
Our father is Abraham.

I have olive skin & dark hair,
I have a Roman nose.
So does my cousin
(I mean the Sephardic one).

But I'm always accused of being anti-Semitic,
Always drilling the point of double jeopardy.
Very confusing to say the least –
I mean you can't tell the two of us apart.
How much you want to bet

That I am a Jew or Arab?
A dollar? Your next paycheck?
The cost of your seat next to me
On a flight to Tel Aviv?
Appearances are deceiving.
Or is it the nose that's doing the magic?

Look at me!
Am I a Jew from the land of Isaac?
Am I Jesus the Nazarene?
Am I Mohammad the Palestinian?
Look to where it all started,
In the land of Canaan, the land of milk and honey.
Of the three of us, no one is safe.

And God said to Moses I AM WHO I AM
AND WHAT I AM AND I WILL BE
WHAT I WILL BE (Exodus 3:14)

All of us dwelled the desert land.
We should go back to God's will
And just get along.
We are cousins since the dawn of time.

Why can't we just talk and clear the air?
Why can't we live side by side?
And stop the bloodshed for crying out loud?
Who's wrong and who's right –
What difference does it make?
Can't we just share the land?
So the world can rest in peace,
And leave us to have peace?
I'm looking for peace of mind.
I hope my cousin is looking as well.
How did it all start?
I wonder how it is going to end.

Child of Peace

I am a child of peace
I think not
I knocked on a door
I tripped on a shaky soil
I struck my head on an olive tree
It did not break
I am a child of peace
I think not
Have seen too many wars
Have wanted peace for ever more
I witnessed blood tattooed on a stone
Have seen broken bones carved on a wall
I tried to open my father's door – in Al-Qatamon
That is West Jerusalem, you know –
They barked at me
'Get lost some more'
I shake no more
I cry no more
I am a child of peace no more
I don't want that 'Right of Return' no more
I don't want that peace signed on a paper, you know
I am a child of peace no more
I do want peace I am sure
I do want my city I am sure
The peace I yearn
Is a peace that never comes?
In a distant land maybe it's there
When a black child and a white child
When a yellow child and a purple child
Play together in harmony
That is peace I want
But the peace I want
Never comes to my nation
No more wars
I am sure I want

With dignity
With real justice
Is the peace I dream about?
I am child of peace
I think not.

Lamenting the Olive Tree

A weeping dove is peeking at me
I gaze into a window of a moving train
I remember mother always saying:
'The more I pray the worse things are deteriorating'

Her tear drop falling down like an icicle on the ground
I try to console her: Mama, things will get eventually better
I always lied to her, she always knew
I also complained to my creator in Silence

I shift into a paradigm and lean on this ugly wall
Snaking through the whole West Bank
With Graffiti decorating one side of that wall
Back to the ghettos

I am still waiting for my lover, she never comes
The fields of tall grass always waving at me
I was born in the raging war and still raging
It's a never-ending cycle of a nightmarish twilight

I will tell suhyun I am back to stay for good
I don't need permission or the world's mercy
I am here and my journey had been long in exile
The birds, my family of 5 million and the Olive Tree are back
The Olive tree that the settler uprooted a thousand times
That tree never left since the last supper of Jesus

I remember,
Chasing my sister in the old city
Visiting mother in a Bedouin town
Praying at the Rock of Ascension
Sitting in the shade of the Olive Tree

I will be reborn into the New Jerusalem
I will meet my lover in an eternal embrace.

A Strange Time

Walk and walk   I feel lost
How are you? Do you feel my pain?
I stand on a very high plateau
On top of the Brooklyn Bridge   awesome view
I observe the human creatures
I observe the East River
I observe and admire nature...
My loved ones why do you accuse me of cruelty
Why do you torture me in this everlasting life?
I asked why the pain?

Do you feel me my love
I have known you since the start of time
I chased you when death came near
And the dark days were all around me
Why do I complain and why do I cry?
Is there anyone out there to hear my screams?
Is there anyone out there that feels
My dire plan and lament...
The place is gone
The time is gone
Time has lapsed   my luck is gone
And it left me behind
How I have wished to have a child of mine
Born in this misery and pain
Maybe my child will not be born
As life is full of sorrow and pain
Maybe my child will not pass in this place
How I wish to meet my child in another time
On another planet in a tranquil galaxy
Maybe I will meet my child in the middle of
Brooklyn Bridge   on Mars or Jupiter
Why do you ask a lot of me?
I do the impossible to please others
I run   I tire

I have to catch my breath
My back is going to break in half from the severe pain
Sometimes I can't stand up straight
But I keep putting on a strong face...
Maybe one day will come   and I will find out
The answer to my existence
Why am I in this universe still breathing?
What am I doing in this place?
What is my goal in this life?
I travel to continents   countries   cities
I take many planes which I hate with a passion
Hoping to find an answer
What is my destiny?
What is my state of mind?
What is my purpose in life?
What am I doing in this world?
Why am I here?
I look around me
I watch the universe unfolding like a machine
The planet is swimming in the mist
Maybe the fog will lift
So I can see my destiny
I look into the horizon
I see the Statue of Liberty
Is that what I want   to be free as a bird?
I am a Palestinian living in a strange land
Maybe my Creator will grant me what I am
Looking for and will liberate my people
So they can live in freedom
No more killings   No more war
No more destruction

Marshland

Standing at the door of a train
I see a line of turtles – 9
Gasping for air
I see an egret worshiping in the distance
Waiting an eternity for that fish
He can never find
From a passing window
On the Passaic river line
That white hope
Standing on one leg all alone
In this GOD forsaken marshland
I see a line of herons – 6
Camouflaged with the brown grass
The evergreen sea of wheat hay
Trying to obstruct my view from
My favorite bird of white haze
Hiding in the shade from a heat wave
In a distant seat of a train
I see this magnetic woman staring me down.

Shaft

Life turning on a needle head
hair spikes up like a porcupine
on a thread
standing my ground
through the ravages
running in a sea of humans
loved ones ignoring
my existence –
I say resistance –
Running all over Palestine
never getting or forgetting
my goal
watching a massacre unfolding
about my nation
under the rubble
under the gun
under siege
bodies decapitated
Zion trying so hard
to erase the 5 percent left over
in utter desolation.
I converse with a stranger
presenting my case.
I bang my fist
on a poster wall
my hand feels no pain.
I ask how I got here.
Mother told me the beginning
I repeat the cycle
again and again
I get back to ground zero.
What is the meaning of this
shafted misery?
I finally realised
I am one drop
in an ocean so deep.

Border Patrol

Crossing over from the Canadian Border
Thousand Islands   the St. Lawrence River Bay
Got pulled over by the Border Patrol
Customs agent stated
You will get back
Your driver's license at the holding station
I asked: *'what's the holding station'?*
Agent just pointed
Go over there
Leave your car
And see the Supervisor
Blonde lady   clicking gum
Angrily asking, *American-born?*
Positive I replied *'YES'*
Supervisor: *I will be right back*
Supervisor returned insisting on the same question
Were you born in the U.S.A?
I stated *now I'm not so sure*
Actually I just remembered   Jerusalem-born
Border patrol – pissed off: *So you are lying*
It's a felony sir to lie to the Border Patrol
After a very long time Border Patrol is back
Don't ever lie to America
'You may go now'
With an attitude and a smile

Destination Unknown

O! Traveller where are you going
I have been to so many places
I have seen too many bloodied humans
In a stone – carved on a wall – splintered on a door
I have seen carnage in the camps

O! Traveller
I wish the future is full of bright white light
I wish my scar will ever heal
I wish my Jerusalem will ever return
I have been denied entry in so many airports
I have been locked up
Indignified – Incinerated – Humiliated
I keep trying again and again

Hoping one day I will reach the shores of Gaza
Allah knows I tried so hard
The many times I joined the Gaza Freedom March
The interviews on TV and radio
Yelling my lungs out
Asking to be back

O! Falasteen
Are you ever coming back?
Or is it
NEVER.

Solitude

I am sinking in a gray fog
It's lifting in Lake Eaton
I am a winner – not a whiner
I regress into a desire of relinquishment
I stumble on a yellow moon
I complain to Akhmatova about my pain
That never heals for 69 years
She cries out
'Still stuck in St. Petersburg's siege of 1942'
Trepidation – solitude & conversations
Twisted in a dark twilight
Running from my destiny
Reading Al-Mutannabi
In City Lore Gallery

The Enemy Came Knocking

The enemy came knocking at my door.
It took me a while, but when my heart stopped racing
I opened the door, after it almost was knocked down.
I asked,
>   *What do you want from me,*
What do you want from my family?
What do you want from my nation?
The victims, the dead are all scattered,
In the hallways, in the hospitals,
Burned in the doorways and the byways,
They are everywhere in the corners.
The enemy yelled at me,
SHUT THE HELL UP!
Don't utter a word.
We ask the stupid questions.
You are nothing,
Your family,
Your Nation is nothing...
We will barge in, force into the place,
We will destroy,
We will erase the time,
We will demolish every living thing.
>   I said,
Why do you want destruction?
Why do you want to kill?
Why do you do what you do?
The enemy said,
Didn't I tell you to shut the hell up?

I am tired of this life; I am tired of this treatment.
The enemy wants to live, but he doesn't want me to breathe
I am a human creature and not an animal.
I am a human & not a building or a house.
I am a human being who has feelings.
I am neither a plant nor an orchard to be bulldozed.

The enemy came
To crush the buildings
To crush the place
To crush my family
To crush and erase my Palestine

The place is gone, the time is lost.
The enemy came knocking at my door.
I asked my Creator, *what is the end?*
My Creator was silent, no word, no whisper, and no clue.

I asked my Creator for help, I heard nothing.
All is lost, all is gone.
Even my Creator is gone.

Delusions

Thinking outward
Talking about building
A permanent trailer
On the other side of the fence
On the other side of the wall
In Bili'n or Nili'n
Asking the settler to get the hell
Out of my home
And move into my tent
The one I'm forced to live in for 64 years
And stop eating my 5% leftover land
A monster is ranting and raving
Like a lunatic
Behind my wall
Paranoid thinking I'm talking
About his stinking wall
Jumping up and down
Pushing and punching me in the eye
'Stop f——-g talking about my WALL'
He barked
Fabricated lies to the superiors
I got banished to a stratosphere
I keep pushing the blue button
The RED one keeps popping up
HELL is breaking loose once more
I don't know if this is the END
Delusional paranoia
The human is famous for
Demilitarized zone
Netanyahu is demanding
So he can finish grabbing the rest of Palestine
Public opinion down the gutter
Mediocre meaningless things
Country gone and now the job in tatters
I keep waiting for a train

To get me to my destination
I do know where
But it's been so long I forgot
One day, I will tell the motorman
My real home, please take me there
And just forget about me.

Nomadic Pilgrimage

I want to go home
I don't know how
I don't know where
I think the land of down under
The Vegemite sandwich
Is it the land of a thousand years?
Where peace never comes
Where the bombs always explode
Where the settlers are burning babies
I am curious to know
Why the world is always silent
I want to go to a land
That doesn't exist
And always resists

Dialogue

Once more, they want to talk
They want to dictate, just to save face
In the western world
They want to cover
The atrocities they commit
The killings of 3 Gazans
Tending to their farm
While they are shooting
A father in East Jerusalem
In cold blood
While the riots are raging
Like brush fire in Bil'n
In Sheikh Jarrah
In the villages of the West Bank
While the settlers confiscate houses
And the owners are living in a tent
While they are demolishing homes
While they are uprooting families
Netanyahu claims Abbas is a partner of peace
I have no idea what Abbas is going to talk about
While Israel is flourishing
Suffocating another nation
They keep the machinery of war stacked
They keep getting more weapons from Uncle Sam
What dialogue are you talking about?
It's just more photo-ups & Armani suits
While Palestine is burning in HELL
We are the Phoenix that rises
From the ashes
Mr. Netanyahu you can talk about that

Do I know you?

At a distance
You feel my pain
I am familiar with your demons
We never met
Yet we are both the same
I talk to the birds
I talk to the olive trees
They have witnessed atrocities
They tell me about genocide
I ask their forgiveness
Let's dance in the poppy seeds
Let's meet in a white world
Let's twirl like Sufi dervishes
Your eyes are Ma'armar
             Your face is A'abhar
                Your look is thunder
We will return to sing and dance
On the streets of Haifa and Gaza
Where the boys hang out on the beach
Without getting bombed
Without getting slaughtered
Without all the F-16's and drones

The Right of Return

My luggage is packed
I always have my bags ready
Ready to go at any time
I have traveled for years
No destination, but one
Always complaining
No one is paying me any attention
No one wants to hear my story
Not even all the Arab World
They choose to ignore me
I landed in Cairo
To go to Gaza under siege
To visit my resisting nation
Mr. Mubarak said 'no can do'
I mean Netanyahu and Obama
Changed his mind
My suitcase on my shoulder
In all of the airports
They call me a terrorist
They keep asking me to leave
And never come back
I always surprise them
By coming back

I don't care
I don't let it get to me
I never listen to anyone
I do what I want
One day will come
I will live in Jericho
Where it all started
And build that home
That I always dreamed of
And start my life
From scratch
After my death in exile
I demand from my land
To be created
So my soul can visit
Happily ever after
Instead of keep visiting
The land of Zion with lots of anger

Baa'ouhaa

the Six Day War 1967

Conspiracy. Confliction. Deterioration. Annihilation.
Refugees in the millions.
Baa'uohaa – they sold the land

I look into the distant land;
I see the Mount of Temptation
Where Jesus fasted for forty days.
I am in a very old land, Jericho,
The oldest city in the world.
Below sea level, home of the Dead Sea.
My childhood city.

Standing at the balcony,
Staring, watching the enemy,
Rolling down,
From the Mount of Temptation
Tanks open fire

I asked my mother,
Why is the man in my house?
Not moving, not breathing –
Is he sleeping?

Mother had nothing to say.
Mother, I asked,
Why is the man bleeding?
Mother, I asked, *what is the man with the army fatigue doing*
Sitting at the corner, with his eyes wide open
Not moving, not walking?
The next day came, and the day after and after.
He is still at the corner, not moving.
He is still staring at my balcony.
Doesn't he need to shut his eyelids?

I was six years old,
I asked all the questions,
Mother didn't have all the answers.

I wore a blue All-Star sneaker,
It was my older brother, Mahmood's sneaker
So large it was bigger than my head.
I still wore it with pride;
It was my favorite brother's sneaker,
It was sacred to me,
I was six years old,
What the hell did I know?

I stepped on to the bus,
My family heading,
Northwest bound, Jerusalem.
The whole world was moving,
Eastbound to the border, Jordan.
The bus driver asked me,
What is this sneaker you're wearing?
And why is it so big on you?
I replied,
My favorite sneaker in the whole wide world –
Baa'ouhaa
The bus driver burst out crying,
And laughing at the same time.
I asked, *Why do you cry,*
It's only my blue All-Star sneaker,
Baa'ouhaa

Ferguson

I am from the south / I am Ferguson
I am a hoot / from the hood
Don't shoot / don't shoot
It's a toy I swear/ it's a toy
Don't worry – don't forget
I am Garner
Don't shove – don't push
I mean the six of you
I can't breathe / I can't breathe
I am not lying / I swear to Allah
I am Amadou reincarnated as Harry
My fifty bullets are healed
Don't frisk me / don't touch me
I know I have an Afro
I am the
Son of de Blasio
The fuzz keeps turning their backs on me
Don't shoot – I am a hoot
God picked my colour
My prayers are with all
But I will never forget.

Al-Shutat

Disaster   dispersed   dismemberment
Displaced but never discarded.
Passing old streets, destroyed houses,
I look for faces from long ago –
Where has everyone gone?
Another day lapses,
And another and another;
Ghosts dwell in the destroyed
Villages of '48.
Exiled all my life, I will return one day
To the garden of my house to see
The Dome of the Rock from my rooftop;
Talk to my neighbour, visit the Indian Hospice,
My family's compound,
Relive memories of the Napalm bombs
That blanketed the place
And burned and killed my family.

I remember water lilies,
The fig and lemon tree.
I once knocked on a door in Al-Qatamon.
A lady answered and shouted,
What do you want!
I replied, *to see my father's house.*
She slammed the door in my face,
It must be another country you're looking for.
I begged her to let me in, screaming,
This is my father's house – I am holding the deed to it!

I passed by the ruins of Hebron's Gate
Where my father's shop once was.
And where the wall of Jerusalem once stood
Has now become No Man's Land.
Why should ghettoes and death camps
Be repeated in Gaza and Jenin?
In Deir Yasin and the Khasin villages of '47?
Why the Haganah's ethnic cleansing
On the northern coast of Palestine?
Expulsions, attacks on local villages?

One day we Palestinians will return
To al-Barweh, Qatamoun,
Deir Yasin, and the Qazaza villages of '48.
Rachel Corrie will be re-born.

My voice will keep circling the skies
So the conscience of the world will hear.
Darwish and Kanafani will resurrect.
The children will not have to starve in Gaza.

No more ethnic cleansing!
No more Balfour Declarations!
No more empty UN resolutions!
No more mass killings of a civilian population!
Simply no more!

I am asking for justice.
I am asking for dignity.
I am asking for my home back.

Remember us.
Keep praying for us.

Ticket to Ride

The beginning started safe
She was crazy about me
We met in Eilat-Red Sea resort
In a swimming pool three in the morning
I called her on the phone
She said:
'Sorry wrong number' and hung up
I was screaming on the other end
'Don't you recognize me'?
'No, I said wrong number' she yelled back
She called an hour later
'I am engaged to be married'
Nadia was a Druze from the Galilee
I am from the forbidden zone.
We met in dark staircases
Under the Mount Carmel
Under the stars of Haifa
Way up near the clouds
Anointing each other's feet
With our sandy tongues
Until the holy war got holier
We had no war between us
Heart to Heart
Palm to Palm
Lips moistened
By our Middle Eastern heat
Nadia was my ticket to ride
Into the Green line and beyond
I am talking about the first Intifada of 1988
The Green line of Jerusalem and far more
It was the war you know
Back to my story
'I am engaged' she said
'Have to do the tribal thing' she was a Druze
She hangs up again for the last time

Never saw her
Never looked for her
But she still plays tricks on my mind
Nadia is her name
Danger element is mine
Che Guevara is my true name.

November 1988

The Horse of Jericho

I am the spirited horse
I gallop over hurdles
I will jump higher
If encouraged

No walls will ever stop me
No checkpoints will deter me
No barbed wires will break me

I am Al Buraq of Mohammad
I am Abu Amar's horse
I am full of ecstasy
I need donations though
From my Saudi & Qatari brothers
Stop sending your money
To buy weapons in Syria that kills
Help me build a better
Equestrian Club in Jericho

I need to compete in the Olympics
I need better conditions in my stables
I am the hope of Palestine
I am the deliverance
I am tired of the wars
I want to have a better life
I tip my hat to Hadeel
I am the horse of Jericho
I am the horse of Palestine

Foot Soldier

for Dareen Tatour

My words are bullets
Mowing down snipers
At the Eretz crossing
At the barbed fence wires
With smoke obstructing
Their view
My words flying over
My land of 48
Of 67
Of a long time ago
Landing on trees
Landing on fields of wheat
My words are detrimental to my enemy
I always speak the truth
Nothing will stop me
Except a bullet
From the IDF

Striker

I am the hunger of days
Living on sea water
Shackled in my dungeon
My thoughts are persistent
Determined to conquer my jailers
Wondering who's over
Who's under?
Deprived basic life
Under bogus detention
No crime committed
I will never surrender
My demands are simple
Use the phone
Get visited
Better food
Definitely be treated as human
Left behind the wall
Left behind barbed wire
My behind is on fire
In the searing heat of the Negev desert
Way down south
No one knows I exist
I always resist
Held in solitary confinement
I am sure my family
The fields
The birds
Are waiting for me
I am a prisoner of conscience
You can chain me
Torture me
Rape me
But you can't break me
I am a prisoner of necessity
Not choice

I will sacrifice my body
Till my enemy succumbs to my demands
No more administrative detention
I mean that Zion
I am Bobby Sands
Ismail Abu Salaama
Nelson Mandela
Rotting in your jails
Kept away
Crossed over
I deserve better
I demand that.

The Storm

Facing Long Lake
Sign 'no swimming'
Storm is coming
Attempted to dip in
Lifeguard yelled at me
'Sir can't you read'
Soon, the gray clouds came
Then the thunder
Then the heavy rains
Washing all that needs to be erased,
Fixing dinner in the soaking woods
Shooting blood rays & purple
Then the calm weather came
The fog covering tips of mountains
Little houses sinking in the mist
Kayaking – rowing straight ahead
Destination 'Smoky Mountains'
Two kroons next to me
One on my right
One on my left
A private escort
Fish jumping up and down
Having a party of a kind
I am one with nature
I am one with Allah
I am one with Lake Eaton
I am praying for my demons to leave me
Tranquility – peaceful intonations
All around me nothing but mist lifting
Looking for peace of mind
Finally I found that moment
Staring into misty lake
After the storm

After the rains
My peace came.

AFTER THE THUNDER
THE BLOOD CAME
AFTER THE RAINS
THE CALM CAME
AFTER THE SUNSHINE
MY PEACE CAME

Journey

Travelling home
11 years passed
Landed in Amman
Where the Bedouins roam
Where I swore never to set foot in
Where the British carved Trans-Jordan

Black September of 1970
Where King Hussein
Bulldozed the camps
I pledged to my comrades in arms
I will avenge their spilled blood

48 years later
I am breaking that promise
To meet two Aunts and an uncle
I have not seen since 67
All that to launch
A Blade of Grass

Poster boy plastered
All over town
King Abdullah not the grandfather
We brought down before
I still reminisce
Al-Karameh of 1968

From My Train Window

I see water moving in haste
An Egret worshiping on his own
Waves in the East River
Having a meeting of a sort
Maybe angry at the ships passing by

I see confiscated horizon
A brother stabbing a brother
After a favor was done in kindness
A man staring in the dark
Harvested civilians in Gaza
& the Mavi Marmara – Turkish boat
Pumped bullets in the chest
Of a Palestinian father in East Jerusalem
Four in the morning by a settler

Houses evacuated in a flash
To make room for settlers from Chicago
While the owners set up a tent outside
Settlers burning the Qur'an in Beit Fajjar
Scrolling graffiti in a Bethlehem mosque
Chaos all over the place
All that while commuting
On the peaceful Jersey line

Twirling Dervish

The birds are looming
in a violet horizon
Horses and feathers
Hamsters and suckers
I am a Sufi dervish
Twirling, calling on
God's ninety-nine names
Soaring above the skies
Of Jerusalem and beyond
The Negev desert
I just want to soar
And reach the unknown
And break away from the shackles
I feel like a prisoner
In a body that does not
Belong to me
I just want to be free
From the entanglements
From the complications
That the human creates
I am still chanting God's names
In the searing desert of my ancestors
Drinking the blood of my invaders
On the Rock of Ascension

Visions of Razan

in memory of Razan Al-Najjar

Gobbling food last minutes of sunrise
Saw a mirage of a kind
30,000 white doves
Soaring above that ugly
Barbed wire fence
Daylight turned night
Under the flying kite
From the bellowing Smokey tires
Birds chirping happy songs
Landing on the erased
Villages of long time ago
Also landing on my demolished
Father's house in what now is
'The Jewish quarter'
Suddenly doves reincarnate
As humans
I glimpsed Razan landing
On her family's house
The nurse who healed
The injured and the passing
That a sniper snuffed her
Life interrupted in the prime
Though she has returned
I landed on my father's demolished house
I forgot, I already said that
But this time
I planted a seed of GRASS.

Resilience

Give me
A teardrop
A mole on my misty cheek
My freedom to set my tears free

Give me
Patience to persevere
An enemy that is brutal
I run in a murky sky
I witnessed ugly atrocities

Give me
Teardrop that will not reach
The asphalt
Till my homeland returns
I pray the slaughtering of the children
Stops
Their blood should not dry
Till Palestine is returned

Give me
A dignified life
Without domination
Free of Nakbah
Free of wars
Never will I give up
My demolished house
Never will I forget Jerusalem
Or Haifa
Or Jaffa
Or Galilee
I keep repeating myself
So I will not forget
Give me
My mother's passion

My father's resilience
I never forget the time
I prayed for mother
In Lake George
In the wintertime frozen town
My tears were falling like icicles.
An egret was keeping me company.

Screaming Olives

Beyond the evergreen
The settler is very mean
The olive tree glimpsed
The oblivious coming
Carrying a tank of petrol
And an M-16 hanging from his shoulder
The branches started waving hurriedly
Then the olives joined in screaming
Like a chorus in a symphony
Call our owners – call our owners
But no comes
Wonder why?
Is it because the soldiers are busy
Sniping the farmers in the harvest
The tree started yelling at the MAN
Get out of my existence
Every time you come, I know I'm gone
Stop killing my babies
Stop suffocating my insides
Stop your savageness...

Emmett Till lynched in 1955
Way down near Selma Alabama
Ali on Grill, the settler taunted
Burned in Duma-West Bank-Palestine in 2015
Mississippi still.

Icy Lake

Driving into nowhere
Fogged up – Visibility   none
Passing Saratoga
The horses
Getting away from betrayal
Bickering and nasty emails
Grieving mother's passing
Fog   somewhat lifting
No end in sight
Entering a dead town
Lake George
Looking at the iced-up lake
Sheets and sheets of thick ice
Grounding the huge tour boats
Individuals crossing the lake on foot
Shuttered windows
Suddenly
A crisp rainbow shows up
A second one right behind
Orange-green-blue and double-purple

Drilling holes
Ice fishing
No fish to catch
God's creation in motion
Trees lined up guarding the lake
Naked like an army guarding
St. Petersburg in Akhmatova's siege in 1941
White and green houses dotting the outskirts
I howling like a wolf
Drinking Vodka to numb the cold and the pain
Tops of mountains with icy frosting
Adirondacks
Drops of gentle rain dropping on my head
Mixed with blood pouring from my hand

Little holes everywhere
Fear of sinking in the ice
Sticks in the head.

Rendition

Landed in an American Airport
Walking in a sea of travelers
Approached by security officers
'Is your name, Anwar El-Ibrahimi?'
'Yes' I replied, 'what is this about?'
'Come with us,' whisked away behind closed doors
Hooded, detained & questioned
Packaged, bundled, put on a private plane
Sent back, return to sender
With escort service of course
Thrown in a dungeon, 3 by 3 hole
Stripped, shackled, tortured a lot more
Water drowning my face,
Hit, spit on, cigarette butts up my ass
'You need to confess to your crimes', they yelled
'But Sir, who are you?'

That's none of your business
But if you insist to know
We are the Rendition Team
We get answers at all cost
We have unlimited access to power & money
We are anonymous
We will disavow any accusations made by you
If you survive, or your family
If they ever find you
Is your real name
Mohamed Farag Ahmad Bashmilah?

Held for years
No charge, no lawyer
No one knows the hell I am in
My father died while detained
My mother put in a mental asylum
Lost my wife and kids...

All in the name of national security!!!
My name is unknown
I lost my life
I have done nothing
Their name is Rendition
Looking for Recognition
America claims democracy
And requires accountability
Obama wants to shut down Guantanamo
After the damage is done
After so many committed suicide
After they put my name in the mud
Obama once said: 'Democracy requires accountability,
And accountability requires transparency'
Human rights ignored, tortured
And severely compromised.
I am a victim in all of this
I have done nothing
I am not waiting for apologies

Not Your Dog

Gaza, under siege for the third year, March 2010

Dear cousin Moshe
You keep shoving the so-
Called peace down my throat
Insisting I should sign that note
Five wars – two Intifadas and now Gaza
You want me to disappear from the Earth
You want me to rat on Hamas
You want me to be a dog like Abbas
To kneel on demand
To shit on command
What kind of peace is that?
My blood is reaching the knee
The other knee is blown out
My boat is stuck in the sand
You even kill the fish
That I need to eat
To make sure you slim me down

YO MOSHE,
When are you ever going to stop?
You and I should go back in time
The Cain & Abel time
But for now, Moshe
Blow up my home
Burn my skin
Cut off my limbs
Keep me a prisoner in my land
Keep throwing stones on my roof
I will never love you back
And as far as Cain and Abel goes
I guess we are all going back
But for now Mr. Chosen Moshe
The souls of Gaza, Shatila and Deir Yassin
Will forever hunt you down...?
I mean haunt you down...

Where Should I Land?

Stranger at the door of hopefulness
Knocking, asking for forgiveness...
My tears soaking the bloody dead
My candle extinguished at dusk...

Flying over strange lands – unknown to me
I am Fatoosh – the flying injured bird –
Searching for HOME
Should I land on God Bless America?
The land of past massacres – Natives
Millions exterminated to make space for another

Or the land of the Euphrates
The land of being reverberated
By again the Bless you America
Or the land of New Zealand
Where East-Meets-West
And nothing much happens
Or the land of Afghanistan
Troop buildup – thank you Obama
Taliban on the rise in Waziristan
Or the Land of Milk and Honey
My ancestors' land
Those idiots that gave up my land
Or the lands of Nepal and Tibet
Once peaceful
And thanks to China – no more

I have been flying for so long
I need to land
I need you to give me permission to land
So I can die peacefully
I mean land peacefully
Before being shot down
By the mighty IDF...

The Visitor

O! Standing erect
I am sad
In my Diaspora
I am sad
In my celebrations
I am sad

O! Flaming apparition
Pour me a drink of blood
I am thirsty
O! Visitor
What is your request?
Is it to enter or leave!!!

Give me peace,
Peace of strength
Not weakness
Are you asking about my wellbeing?

Give me serenity
O! Dear one
Asking about the universe or what?
Why do you come to my dreams?

O! Father
How are you?
Do you come to ask about my mother?
And can I see you again?

Man-handled

Go back   Go back
Travelling on the Commuter Jersey Line
Go back   Go back
Sonny just Go back
To the war raging
In Gaza land – In Jenin
To the graveyards of
Sabra & Shatila – Deir Yassin
Go back   Go back
Where home is – Was and Will
Got Bunt headed by a commuter
Pushed the Adam away
He took me down Karate style
Landed on the seats
Blood pouring from my arm
He yelled *stay down stay down*
Stumped on my chest to keep me down
Sprung back up
I am not a dog to stay down
Got some more beating
While I was fighting back
Car emptied out
No one to lend a hand
Four cops barging in
Both of you come on out
they barked. *Fuzz are scum,*
You deserve what you got.

I'd rather go back
To the war raging land
Where I belong
Where safety is
Where warmth is plenty
Than to be manhandled
          Mishandled
             Mistreated
And abused on the tranquil Jersey line...

Homeland

You birthed me
        You gave me
                You suffocated me
                        Yet, I still smell you...
In the Jasmine & Qurunful
In the streets of Gaza-Jenin-Nablus
Thirty years in exile
My umbilical cord
Still connected to you
I still dream of the casabas
I still dream of the Dome of the Rock
I still see the IDF soldiers
From my window
Breaking bones – Stealing
Killing civilians with their M-16's
My name is everywhere I travel
In every Airport
In every police station
I am famous all over town
I always ask:
What have I done?
To deserve all the notoriety
The whole world thinks
I am a destroyer
In actuality
I am a lover – misunderstood...

HOMELAND
Give me hope
Give me sweet days again
Give me rivers of Banyas.
You told me,
You will come back one day,
You lied to me, you lied to me.
I am still waiting for you
I am tired of tick-tock... waiting-waiting
Ya Mawtini... A'ashiqun- A'ashiqun...

Eternity and a Day

'don't hurry the journey at all.
Better if it lasts for years,
so you're old by the time you reach the island,
wealthy with all you've gained on the way.'
C.P. Cavafy, 'Ithaka'

Ithaca has not deceived –
      Ithaca is rich and not poor

How long does tomorrow last?

If I could only hold the moment
     So I can pin it on my chest

Like a Butterfly Butterfly, you fly!

Korfula my flower dies
      In the desert

The wind takes your eyes
     Far away

I hear the footsteps
      Echoing in my house
Sobrecho Vassilis Khristos

Now I face the sea
     There is no end to it

Why have I lived my life in exile?
     Why must we rot in this life?

Or retrieve lost words from
  Silence

How long does tomorrow last?
  Argadini

It's very late

I stand here and
                    Wait for you trembling

I wait for you by the sea

The Poet asked
How long does tomorrow last?

His lover said
An eternity and a day

Korfula   Korfula   Moo

I stand facing the sea
  Today is my day

Today is eternity and a day

Broken Down

At the Rafah crossing
Stepping into a war zone
A man sitting in a corner
Face ageless
Features unknown
I sat next to the man
Broken Down – Broken Down
Obscure objects
At the Rafah border town
A war zone left behind
Hundreds of broken-down homes
Bloodied eyes
From crying over children
Destroyed lives at the Eretz crossing
Private escort into the narrow streets
Of Rafah town
Huddled in a guest house
A man spilling his guts out
About his demolished building
15 years of savings
Gone in a flash – in a flash
By the IDF soldiers
To make room for a better view
A man living in a rented house
For the third time
Sharing pictures of his
Long gone home
Israeli snipers shooting
Anything moving
Shooting fish in a barrel – fish in a barrel
A broken-down man
With tears in his eyes
Didn't know what to tell the MAN
Jobless – Homeless – and now Broken Down.

Uprooted Trees

From my train window
I watch buildings going backward
In the reflection
The river is confused
I avoid looking into faces unknown to me
From my home window
I hear a large bang – five in the morning
Uprooted tree, falling on my neighbours' house
What a scary sight
It could have been my bedroom window
The next day
Another huge tree
Decided to commit suicide as well
It's missing its sister
Shattering two brand new cars
My quiet street looks
Like a War Zone
Electricity gone for days
Food rotting in the houses
No computer, TV or ipad
Going back to simpler times
Takes me back to camping days
Nosey neighbours hanging out
I want to move out of this toxic town
To a house on a hill
Facing a lake
Glass all around
In no man's land
I want to go back to simpler times
My street looks like a scene from
GAZA TOWN...

Only Stones Remain

During the 52-day invasion of Gaza 2,185 civilians were killed
by the Israeli Defence Force

again and again
falling down on my head
and the dead are too many
to blame
only stones remain
Umm Ahmad wailing
holding a stone in one hand
hitting her face with the other
screaming,
where is my beautiful house
where is my beautiful life
where is my son I am looking for
I have his favourite toy
I found his arms
I found his legs
I can't find his head
where is my beautiful child
where is my beautiful wife
where is my beautiful house
I am not talking about
talking heads
only stones remain
again and again
falling down on my head
I will rebuild Shuja'aiya
I will rebuild every stone
I will rebuild Beit Hanoun
that al-shaytan Zion destroyed

and the dead are too
many to blame.

27 August 2014

To My Jerusalem

City of my birth, my memories of you
are both pleasant and painful.
I still run in the narrow streets of the Old City
along walls centuries old, built by
Salah Ad-Din, vanquisher of the Crusaders.

I walk the Via Dolorosa, in the footsteps of Jesus.
I enter the Dome of the Rock,
where Muhammad ascended to the seven skies.
I still follow in my father's footsteps
as he heads for his shop –
narrow alleys, streets, and entrances,
the smell of jasmine and honeysuckle,
souqs, souvenir shops, and countless markets:
the spice market, the copper market,
meat market, sweets market...
Faces seen day in day out
in the tiny hummus and falafel cafes,
the family butcher carving our favorite
cuts of meat for Eid...
Memories of me running to the market
for my mother's missing ingredients,
the smell of fresh coffee,
the coal burner in winter,
barbeque in spring,
and images of my mother
tending plants in the garden,
visiting the holy places – Omar's Mosque,
the Holy Sepulchre,
stores, houses, bakeries...

I remember well the air raid sirens, too,
October's War, 1973 – the Yom Kippur War,
fighter jets thundering in the sky, bombs exploding
as my brother and I run to safety.
The look of fear on my mother's face,
the blackened windows, shuttered shops during curfew time.
I remember the anger of the Zionist enemy after the war.
I remember the demonstrations against the occupation.
I remember the fallen victims resisting the occupier.
I remember the happiness of the nation as the enemy was losing.

Then I remember better days,
when I played marbles in the dirt.
When I walked to school every day,
bought a shawarma sandwich
and drank 7 Up with my mother.
My beloved Jerusalem,
You live in my soul.
You live in my dreams.

Nakbah

15 May 1948–6 June 1967

I have told this story

So many versions
That sometimes I forget
How it all started
An eternity away
Mother narrated the middle
I read the start

Father refrained from talking
I keep dwelling on the past
While I should build the future
The problem is
Every time I build the nest
Zion keeps destroying it

It all started a simple way
An innocent child
Growing in a sleepy town – Jericho
I still remember the mint tea
I still smell the rain evaporating.

Flying Bird

Lemon Tree
Olive Tree
Fig Tree...

I am transforming,
I am a shapeshifter
In a leap of faith
Upside down Life
Horizon – New
Constricted – conflicted
But committed...

Star formation,
In another galaxy,
Red room,
Pinot-Grigio,
Watching the waves...

I am,
The flying bird of Palestine.
I am,
Al-Anbar, Khandahar,
Blue water surging,
Troop build-up,
And the trees blowing...

The Jerusalem Drum

performed on the tablas

Born in   a Holy Land
Born, I was born in
A land that knows
No peace
Old city
Where prophets walked
And memories burn...
Land of a thousand eyes
That never sleeps
And always weeps
In my veins
My childhood boy
Runs in the sand
Naked as a bird
Free in my soul
Above the Earth
Where the bombs explode...

Allah Ha'ie Allah Ha'ie...

Notes

Above the Clouds
The Umayyad dynasty were the ruling family of the Muslim caliphate 661–750 CE, and later of Islamic Spain 756–1031 CE. Tareq ibn Ziyad led the Muslim conquest of Spain. In 2010, Farid Bitar took part in a protest outside New York's Waldorf Astoria Hotel, where Israeli Defence Force Chief of Staff Gabi Ashkenazi was speaking at a fund-raising dinner.

Handalah
Naji al-Ali was a Palestinian cartoonist assassinated in London in 1987. Although no-one was ever convicted of the murder, the UK government subsequently closed the London offices of Mossad and expelled three Israeli diplomats. A sabra is a prickly pear; the term is also used to refer to Jews born in Israel (including the Occupied Territories). Handalah is the name of Naji al-Ali's most famous cartoon character. After his death, Handalah became a popular symbol of Palestinian oppression and resistance. The name is derived from a watermelon-like plant local to Palestine; it bears a bitter fruit, has deep roots and always grows back when cut.

Upstream
Selma, Alabama, was a centre of the US Civil Rights movement in the 1960s. When Martin Luther King tried to lead a Civil Rights march from Selma to Montgomery in 1965, the marchers were violently assaulted by State Troopers.

Hicks Town
'Shika Beeka' means 'Shake and Bake'.

Red Red–Green Green
In November 2012, Israeli forces invaded Gaza. George Habash was secretary general of the Popular Front for the Liberation of Palestine from 1967–2000. Ahmed Jibril is the founder and leader of the breakaway Popular Front for the Liberation of Palestine – General Command.

Vision of Hope
Black September refers to the fighting between the Jordanian army and the PLO in September 1970, which left 25k Palestinian dead. 'Falasteen' means Palestine.

Return
'Şahyun' is the word for Zion in Arabic.

Knocking
The Balfour Declaration in 1917 committed the British government to establishing a 'national home' for the Jewish people.

Who Am I?
'Al-Tadd-hiyha' means the sacrifice.

Destination Unknown
The Gaza Freedom March was a planned protest in 2009 against the blockade of the Gaza Strip by the Israeli government.

Solitude
Al-Mutannabi was a tenth-century Arabic poet.

The Enemy Came Knocking
The First Intifada (1987-1992), sometimes known as the 'Stone Intifada', was a civilian uprising against the Israeli occupation of the West Bank and Gaza. During the Intifada, an estimated 1.2k Palestinians were killed by the IDF.

Delusions
The West Bank villages of Nili'n and Bili'n are the focus for weekly protests against the Wall.

Dialogue
In 2010 the Obama administration began peace talks with the Israeli government and the Palestinian Authority, with the aim of reaching a 'two-state solution'.

Baaʾouhaa
'Baaʾouhaa' means 'they sold it'.

Ferguson
In 2014, 18 year-old Michael Brown Jr was fatally shot by a policeman in Ferguson, Missouri. A month earlier Eric Garner died in New York while being arrested and held in a prohibited chokehold. He repeated the words 'I can't breathe' several times before losing consciousness. Amadou Diallo was shot and killed in 1999 by New York police in a case of 'mistaken identity'.

Al-Shutat
'Al-Shutat' means dispersed or shattered. The Haganah was a Jewish paramilitary organization in Palestine from 1920 until 1948, when it became the core of the IDF. Al-Barweh, Al-Qatamoun, Deir Yasin, and Qazaza were Palestinian villages before 1948. Rachel Corrie was an American member of the pro-Palestinian International Solidarity Movement; she was killed in 2003 by an IDF armoured bulldozer in Gaza, while protesting at the demolition of Palestinian houses. The writer Mahmoud Darwish (1941–2008) was often described as the Palestinian national poet. Ghassan Kanafani (1936–1972) was a Palestinian novelist and a leading member of the PFLP; he was assassinated by Mossad in 1972.

The Horse of Jericho
Al Buraq carried Mohammed from Mecca to Jerusalem.

Striker
In 2017, 1500 political Palestinian prisoners went on hunger strike for 40 days. In 1972 Ismail Abu Salaama was given seven life-sentences for being a member of the PFLP; while in prison, he was involved in a hunger strike in 1980. He was eventually released in a prisoner-exchange in 1985.

From My Train Window
In 2010, a mosque in Beit Fajjar near Bethlehem was attacked by Jewish settlers opposed to a peace deal between Israel and the Palestinians, burning the Koran and scrawling threats in Hebrew on the walls.

Visions of Razan
Razan Al-Najjar was a Palestinian nurse killed by the Israeli Defence Force during the Gaza border protests in 2018; she was shot while evacuating the wounded near Israel's border fence with Gaza.

Screaming Olives
Emmett Louis Till was a 14-year-old African-American; he was lynched in Mississippi in 1955 after being accused of offending a white woman. 'Ali on the Grill' refers to 18-month year-old Ali Saad Dawabshe, who was killed with his parents when Jewish settlers firebombed the family home in the West Bank in 2015. At the trial, surviving members of the family were taunted by crowds chanting 'Ali on the grill'. The poet Dareen Tatour was convicted in 2018 in an Israeli court for 'inciting violence' in a poem about the murders ('So Ali called from his grave, resist, my people, resist them').

Rendition
In the US film *Rendition* (2007), Anwar El-Ibrahimi is kidnapped by the CIA, flown overseas and tortured. Mohamed Farag Ahmad Bashmilah was kidnapped and tortured for two years in extrajudicial detention in the CIA's network of 'black' sites.

Homeland
'Ya Mawtini' means my homeland. 'A'ashiq-in' means to be in love.

Broken Down
This poem was written on a visit to Rafah in Gaza, in January 2010.

Only Stones Remain
Shuja'aiya is a district of Gaza city. In 2015 the area was heavily shelled by Israeli forces; between 65 and 120 Palestinians were killed in the fighting, including at least 17 children. Beit Hanoun is a city in the Gaza strip. 19 Palestinian civilians died there as a result of shelling by the IDF. The United Nations appointed a fact-finding commission led by Desmond Tutu, to investigate if the shelling constituted a war crime; the investigation was cancelled due to the lack of Israeli cooperation. Al-shaytan is the devil.

Nakbah
Al-Nakbah ('disaster') refers to the exodus of over 700k Palestinians who fled or were expelled from their homes in 1948.

The Jerusalem Drum
'Allah Ha'ie' means 'God is alive'.

Acknowledgements

Thanks are due to the editors of the following publications, where some of these poems have previously been published: *Critical Muslim, Poetry Bay* and Naomi Foyle (ed) *A Blade of Grass: New Palestinian Poetry* (Smokestack Books, 2017).